Flute Solo • Piano

O Holy Night

A Christmas Collection for Flute & Piano

ARRANGED BY KAREN SMITH AND DAVID SNYDER

PLAYBACK+
Speed • Pitch • Balance • Loop

To access audio visit:
www.halleonard.com/mylibrary

Enter Code
5199-3033-8204-4433

ISBN 978-1-4234-8941-2

HAL•LEONARD®
CORPORATION

7777 W. BLUEMOUND RD. P.O. BOX 13819 MILWAUKEE, WI 53213

Visit Hal Leonard Online at
www.halleonard.com

ANGELS WE HAVE HEARD ON HIGH

Traditional
Arranged by Karen Smith
and David Snyder

AWAY IN A MANGER

Traditional
Arranged by Karen Smith
and David Snyder

27 More Broadly

CHRISTMAS CAROL SUITE

Arranged by Karen Smith
and David Snyder

5 "Joy to the World"

"The Twelve Days of Christmas"

Reverently (♩ = 60)

"We Wish You a Merry Christmas"

DECK THE HALL VARIATIONS

Traditional
Arranged by Karen Smith
and David Snyder

GESÙ BAMBINO
(The Infant Jesus)

By PIETRO YON
Arranged by Karen Smith
and David Snyder

IT CAME UPON THE MIDNIGHT CLEAR / SILENT NIGHT

Arranged by Karen Smith
and David Snyder

Lyrically, poco rubato
"It Came Upon the Midnight Clear"
By RICHARD S. WILLIS

JESU, JOY OF MAN'S DESIRING

By JOHANN SEBASTIAN BACH
Arranged by Karen Smith
and David Snyder

LO, HOW A ROSE E'ER BLOOMING

15th Century German Carol
Arranged by Karen Smith
and David Snyder

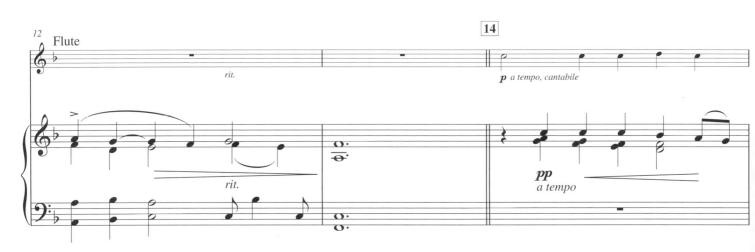

O HOLY NIGHT

By ADOLPHE ADAM
Arranged by Karen Smith
and David Snyder

THREE CAROLS IN 6/8 TIME

Arranged by Karen Smith
and David Snyder

82 "Bring a Torch, Jeanette, Isabella"

WE THREE KINGS OF ORIENT ARE

By JOHN H. HOPKINS, JR.
Arranged by Karen Smith
and David Snyder

WHAT CHILD IS THIS? / COVENTRY CAROL

Arranged by Karen Smith
and David Snyder